SPIES AND SPYING

KATE **WALKER** I ELAINE **ARGAET**

This edition first published in 2004 in the United States of America by Smart Apple Media.

Smart Apple Media
1980 Lookout Drive
North Mankato
Minnesota 56003

Library of Congress Cataloging-in-Publication Data

Walker, Kate.
   Super spies of World War I / by Kate Walker & Elaine Argaet
   v. cm — (Spies and spying)

   Includes index.
   Contents: Baden-Powell, the Boy Scout spy—Mata Hari, the 'eye of the day'—Karl Lody, the inexperienced spy—Edith Cavell, the soldier's nurse—Lawrence of Arabia, the desert spy—Louise de Bettignies, the spy who hid things well—Sidney Reilly, the spy with many masters—Julius Silber, the perfect spy—Maria de Victorica, the South American spy queen—Franz von Rintelen, the mad bomber—Marthe Richer, double agent—Wilhelm Wassmuss, the golden spy—Elspeth Schragmuller, the spy teacher.

   ISBN 1-58340-339-6
   1. World War, 1914–1918—Secret service—Juvenile literature. 2. Spies—Biography—Juvenile literature.
   3. Espionage—History—20th century—Juvenile literature. [1. World War, 1914–1918—Secret service.
   2. Spies. 3. Espionage—History—20th century.] I. Argaet, Elaine. II. Title. III. Series.
   D639.S7W34 2003
   940.54'85'0922—dc21
   [B]   2002044623

First Edition
9 8 7 6 5 4 3 2 1

First published in 2003 by
MACMILLAN EDUCATION AUSTRALIA PTY LTD
627 Chapel Street, South Yarra, Australia, 3141

Associated companies and representatives throughout the world.

Edited by Miriana Dasovic
Text and cover design by Marta White
Maps and illustration on page 7 by Pat Kermode, Purple Rabbit Productions
Photo research by Jes Senbergs

Printed in Thailand

Acknowledgements

The author and the publisher are grateful to the following for permission to reproduce copyright material:

Cover photograph: Mata Hari, and magnifying glass, courtesy of Getty Images; eye, courtesy of Ingram Royalty Free Image Library.

Archiv Gerstenberg, p. 25 (bottom); Australian Picture Library/Corbis, pp. 9, 11 (bottom), 23, 25 (top), 29 (bottom); Bilder Süddeutscher, p. 11 (top); Getty Images, pp. 1, 3, 4, 5, 6, 8, 13 (top), 15, 18, 19 (bottom), 32 (all); Ingram Royalty Free Image Library, pp. 1 (eye), 7 (center), 10, 17, 27 (bottom right); *London Illustrated News*, p. 21 (top); Roger Viollet, p. 26; The Trustees of the Imperial War Museum, London, p. 21; Ullstein Bild Berlin, p. 28.

While every care has been taken to trace and acknowledge copyright, the publisher tenders their apologies for any accidental infringement where copyright has proved untraceable. Where the attempt has been unsuccessful, the publisher welcomes information that would redress the situation.

CONTENTS

INTRODUCTION

Mata Hari, one of the most famous spies in the world.

What is a spy?

A spy is a person who deals in secret information. Some spies gather the information, usually by sly means. Other spies carry the information from one person to another. There are spies who sit at desks and study the information, while other spies go out into the field and act on it. Some spies make up false information and spread it around to fool the enemy. Anyone who works secretly in this way is a spy.

- ◉ The proper name for spying is espionage.
- ◉ The modern name for a spy is an agent or intelligence officer.
- ◉ Information gathered by spies is called intelligence.

When did spying start?

People have been spying on each other since human history began. Army leaders have always known that the best way to defeat an enemy is to find out that enemy's weakness, and the best person to discover that weakness is a spy.

Why do people become spies?

Sometimes people become spies out of loyalty to their country. They gather information that will help keep their country safe. Sometimes people become spies because they know important secret information and sell it for money, usually a lot of money. Some people are tricked or forced into becoming spies. Other people choose to become spies because they find it exciting.

World War I begins

World War I began on July 28, 1914. It started when Austria invaded Serbia, and Germany invaded Belgium. The war was fought mainly between two groups of countries in Europe. One group was called the Central Powers. It included Austria–Hungary, Germany, Bulgaria, and Turkey. The other group was called the Allied Powers, or Allies. It included Britain, France, Italy, Greece, and Russia. The United States, Canada, Australia, and New Zealand helped the Allied Powers by sending food, weapons, and troops to Europe.

Who used spies?

Countries on both sides of the war used spies. For the first time in Western history, spies were trained. However, most spies were not trained very well. Many German spies sent to England could not speak English.

Simple spying

Spies used a few simple gadgets. They wrote messages in invisible ink, and used simple codes and ciphers. Some spies traveled around on bicycles. Others sent messages by carrier pigeon. Some of the most famous spies in the world operated during this war. The most famous were Lawrence of Arabia, Mata Hari, and Sidney Reilly.

World War I ended on November 11, 1918.

Lawrence of Arabia worked as a spy during World War I.

ciphers	secret languages that hide words by jumbling their letters
codes	secret languages
gadgets	special tools
into the field	going into other countries to spy
invaded	used force to enter someone else's land

BADEN-POWELL, THE BOY SCOUT SPY

BACKGROUND

- Ten years before World War I started, Austria and Turkey began building stronger forts.

- It looked like they were getting ready for war, so Britain began spying on them.

Baden-Powell founded the Boy Scout movement in 1908.

Robert Baden-Powell: 1857–1941
Born: London, England
Spied for Britain against the Central Powers

Born to be a spy

Robert Baden-Powell had to pass an entrance exam to join the army. His exam marks were very high, so he was not sent for ordinary army training. Instead, he began work as an army intelligence officer. He soon became spy chief for the whole Mediterranean area.

A spying vacation

As a spy chief, Baden-Powell continued to spy even when he was on vacation. Once, he was on a steamship going up the narrow straits of the Dardanelles. There were Turkish forts on either side, and Baden-Powell wanted to get a closer look at them. He asked the steamship captain to help. The steamer stopped, and Baden-Powell got into a small rowboat and rowed towards one of the forts. A Turkish patrol boat came along to see why the steamer had stopped. At that moment, a workman in the engine room began hammering loudly. The captain told the Turks that the ship's engine had stalled and was being repaired. Meanwhile, Baden-Powell sat in his small rowboat pretending to fish. He was really sketching the details of the forts.

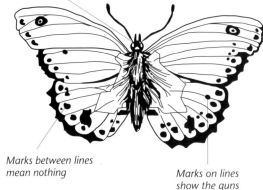

The sketch

Butterfly head always points north

Marks between lines mean nothing

Marks on lines show the guns

The plan hidden inside the sketch

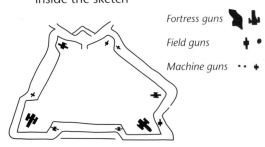

Fortress guns

Field guns

Machine guns

Collecting butterflies

Baden-Powell's main job as spy chief was to find out the military strength of the Austrians. He needed to know how many guns were in a particular fort on the coast of the Adriatic Sea. To find out, he took a butterfly net and a sketchbook and climbed right up to the walls of the fort. There Baden-Powell wandered about catching butterflies. After a while, he sat down and began to draw pictures of the butterflies in his sketchbook.

The Austrian guards came down from the fort to see what he was doing. Baden-Powell showed them his butterfly sketches. He asked the guards if they had seen butterflies like the ones he had drawn. The guards said they knew nothing about butterflies. Baden-Powell was pleased. This meant he could carry on drawing his picture of the fort, which was hidden inside the pattern on the butterfly's wings.

Baden-Powell sketched an outline of the fort in the pattern on the butterfly's wings. The marks between the lines on the wings meant nothing, but the marks made on top of the lines showed the guns. The lines on which the marks occurred indicated the location of the guns inside the fort. The size of the guns was shown by a simple code of shapes. The butterfly's head pointed north.

| military | the armed forces |
| spy chief | a person in charge of other spies |

MATA HARI, THE "EYE OF THE DAY"

BACKGROUND

- Some countries did not join in the fighting in World War I. They stayed neutral.

- Holland (now called the Netherlands) and Spain were two countries that stayed neutral.

- A person from a neutral country was not treated as an enemy, unless they were a spy.

Margaretha Zelle, known as **Mata Hari**: 1876–1917
Born: Leeuwarden, Holland
Spied for Germany against France

Fame

Mata Hari married at 18 and went to live in Java. There she learned to dance in the beautiful Javanese style. When she returned to Holland in 1902, Mata Hari became an entertainer. Her unusual dancing style made her famous. Important people flocked to see her. For the next 10 years, Mata Hari lived an exciting and glamorous life. She traveled through France, Spain, and Germany. Many people said she was the most beautiful woman in Europe.

Mata Hari, spy

When World War I broke out in 1914, Mata Hari was living in Berlin. Her friend, the German chief of police, asked her to spy for Germany. He gave her invisible ink for writing secret messages. Mata Hari went to France. She mixed with French military officers and charmed military secrets out of them. One day, French police came to see Mata Hari and told her they knew what she was doing. Mata Hari was frightened, and offered to switch sides. She would spy for the French instead.

Mata Hari dancing in a Javanese costume. The name Mata Hari is a Javanese phrase meaning "the eye of the day."

Mata Hari, double agent

The French sent Mata Hari into Belgium to get information from German military officers. They gave her a list of other French spies to contact. One of these French spies was arrested by German secret police two weeks later. The French thought that Mata Hari had betrayed him. The Germans too thought that Mata Hari was a double agent working for the French. She was in grave danger and had to get away.

Warned to give up spying

Mata Hari sailed to England. There she was questioned by Sir Basil Thomson, a British police chief. He warned Mata Hari that she was not very good at spying and should give it up. At first it looked like she took his advice. Mata Hari did not go back to Germany. Instead, she sailed for Spain. However, she soon contacted German agents again and crossed into France on yet another spy mission.

Wrongly blamed

Mata Hari was immediately arrested by French police. Ink for writing secret messages was found in her bag. The war had been going badly for the French. Mata Hari was someone they could blame. They wrote newspaper stories saying that she was the greatest spy of all time and had stolen French military secrets. On October 15, 1917, Mata Hari was taken to the moat of the Chateau de Vincennes outside Paris. She was given a glass of brandy and shot.

Ultraviolet light reveals the use of invisible ink on an innocent-looking letter.

double agent   a spy pretending to work for one country while secretly working for another

KARL LODY, THE INEXPERIENCED SPY

BACKGROUND

? When World War I started in 1914, the British secret service arrested every known German spy in Britain.

? Germany quickly had to send more spies to take their place.

Karl Lody: 1879–1914
Born: Berlin, Germany
Spied for Germany against Britain

Early jobs

Karl Lody was in the German navy until 1900. Then he got a job as a tour guide on an American ocean liner. Lody sailed around the world showing rich tourists the sights. In 1914, he could see that war was coming, so he left his tour ship and went home to Germany. His plan was to rejoin the navy so he could fight for his country. Lody spoke perfect English. He was just the sort of person the Germans wanted as a spy, or so they thought.

Sent to Britain as a spy

Lody was given a few weeks of spy training and a false American passport. He sailed for Scotland and arrived in Edinburgh in September 1914. Lody's job was to find out how many warships were in the British fleet. He rented a room in Edinburgh and rented a bicycle. Lody set off cycling around the Firth of Forth, a large inlet off the North Sea. In this inlet, Lody found most of the British fleet riding at anchor. He counted the number of warships and sent a telegram to his spy chief in Europe.

North Sea
Scotland
Edinburgh · Firth of Forth
BRITAIN
Ireland · Liverpool
England
Mersey River · London
Berlin ·
GERMANY

N

0 100 200 300 miles

Karl Lody in his naval uniform.

Interested in warships and guns

Lody knew very little about being a spy. He did not try to hide his interest in the warships, and asked the local Scottish people questions about them. The local people thought this was suspicious, so they reported Lody to the police. British secret service agents were soon following Lody. All the telegrams he sent to his spy chief in Europe were stopped by the British post office. One week later, Lody realized that he was being followed and he left Scotland. He disappeared for a while, but was spotted again at a military base in southern England. Once more, he was asking local people questions about the base and its guns.

Secretly watched

Secret service agents followed Lody day and night. They wanted to see where he would go, what he would do next, and who he would contact. Next, Lody went to Liverpool. He drew sketches of the guns along the Mersey River. In Liverpool, he boarded a ship bound for Ireland. Moments before the ship sailed, the British police arrested Lody. His short spying career lasted just five weeks. None of the information he gathered ever reached Germany.

Lody was imprisoned in the Tower of London, and a military court found him guilty of spying. He was the first spy to be executed by the British in World War I.

The Tower of London, where Lody was imprisoned and executed.

inlet a strip of water stretching into the land from the sea

ocean liner a luxury passenger ship

passport an official identification document needed by someone traveling to another country

secret service another name for a spy network

EDITH CAVELL, THE SOLDIERS' NURSE

BACKGROUND

- Belgium was a small, neutral country.

- Thousands of German troops invaded Belgium in August 1914 in the space of just a few days.

- British soldiers stationed in Belgium were forced to retreat. Many were stranded behind enemy lines.

Hospital matron

Edith Cavell was matron of a training school for nurses in Brussels. When Germany invaded Belgium, wounded soldiers from both sides were brought to Cavell's hospital for treatment. She told her nurses that they had to care for all the soldiers, whether they were German or British.

The first two soldiers Cavell saved

One wet night in November 1914, two British soldiers disguised as workmen arrived at the hospital. One had a wounded leg. Both men were dirty and tired. Cavell kept them hidden in the hospital for two weeks. She feared what would happen to them if they were found by the Germans. A soldier caught behind enemy lines who was not wearing a uniform was assumed to be a spy, and could be shot. With the help of Belgian friends, Cavell had the two soldiers moved from house to house until they finally reached the Dutch border. Under cover of darkness, the two men dashed across the border to safety.

Matron Edith Cavell (second row, center) with some of her student nurses in Brussels.

Escape chain

Cavell became part of an escape chain that helped 200 British, French, and Belgian soldiers get safely out of Belgium. This escape chain included lawyers and farmers, nuns and priests—even a prince. The network of helpers hid soldiers in their cellars and barns. They gave them clothes and false identity cards. At night they guided the soldiers down cobbled streets or across fields, from one safe house to the next.

The list of names

Cavell was told by friends that the Germans had become suspicious of her. She was warned to leave Belgium. Other nurses heeded the warning and left. Cavell felt that it was her duty to stay. In August 1915, German police raided the home of a member of the escape chain and found a suspicious list of names. Cavell's name was on the list. She was arrested and her hospital was searched. The Germans found nothing. Cavell kept a secret diary in which she wrote about everything she did, but it was safely sewn inside a cushion.

THE STORY OF Edith Cavell

BY IRIS VINTON
ILLUSTRATED BY GE...

The cover of a book telling of the brave deeds of Edith Cavell.

Cavell confesses

Thirty-five members of the escape chain were arrested. The German officer who questioned Cavell told her that the others had confessed. This was a trick to get her to admit her guilt, and she did. On the morning of October 12, 1915, Edith Cavell was executed by firing squad. She died wearing her nurse's uniform.

disguised   when a person's appearance is changed so they look like someone else

Dutch   belonging to Holland

identity cards   official cards with a person's name and photograph that prove who they are

matron   person in charge of nurses in a hospital

LAWRENCE OF ARABIA, THE DESERT SPY

Thomas Edward Lawrence: 1888–1935
Born: Wales, Britain
Spied for Britain against Turkey

BACKGROUND

By 1914, Turkey had ruled Arabia for more than 400 years.

When World War I started, the Turks were busy fighting the British. The Arabs saw their chance to rise up and take back their homeland.

Lawrence's first spy mission

T.E. Lawrence came to Arabia when he was 20 years old to work on archaeological diggings. The British government asked the members of the diggings team if they would make secret maps of the Arabian countryside and spy on the towns. One of these towns was on an island near Akaba. Lawrence swam out to the island using his camel's waterbag as a float.

A friend to the Arabs

Lawrence liked the Arab people, and quickly became friends with their leaders. He spoke their language, ate their food, and became an expert camel rider. In the desert, he wore flowing Arabian clothes.

Divide and conquer

When World War I started, Lawrence joined the British army. The British were fighting the Turks in Palestine, and this gave Lawrence an idea. He offered to organize the different Arab tribes into one army and lead them against the Turks in the Sinai Desert. This would force the Turks to divide their army and fight a war on two fronts.

N

TURKEY

Mediterranean Sea

PALESTINE

Deraa

Sinai Desert

Akaba

The Gulf

Red Sea

ARABIA

EGYPT

0   250   500   750 miles

Guns and gold

Lawrence met with Arab leaders in their tents. He told them that if they were willing to band together to fight the Turks, he would give them British guns and gold. The Arabs agreed. Lawrence traveled with them through the desert, helping them make daring raids behind Turkish lines. They wrecked bridges and blew up trains. The Arabs were good at this sort of fighting. It helped cut off the Turks' line of supply.

Dangerous work

One time, Lawrence sneaked into the town of Deraa late at night. Before his Arab troops attacked, he wanted to see how strong the Turkish forces were. He wore Arab clothes but could not hide his blue eyes. Lawrence was spotted as a British spy and captured. He was tortured by the Turkish commander but did not give the Turks any information, not even his name. When he was left unguarded for a moment, he escaped.

Arabia is given to the French

When the war ended, Britain let the French take control of the land for which the Arabs had fought. Lawrence was so angry that he left the British army. When the king of England presented Lawrence with a medal for bravery, Lawrence politely refused. He never forgave the British for misleading him and his Arab friends.

Lawrence in his Arabian clothes.

A Turkish train blown up by Lawrence's Arab fighters.

archaeological diggings   places where ancient cities are dug up and studied

line of supply   route along which supplies are transported

LOUISE DE BETTIGNIES, THE SPY WHO HID THINGS WELL

BACKGROUND

? Germany invaded northern France in August 1914.

? Thousands of French people sailed across the English Channel, seeking safety in Britain.

Louise de Bettignies: 1880–1918
Born: Lille, France
Spied for France and Britain against Germany

A keen eye for detail

Louise de Bettignies arrived in England from France in 1914 and gave British customs officers valuable information about the German army. Bettignies had a good eye for detail. She also spoke English, French, and German. She was of small build and was 34 years old. The British asked if she would return to France and spy for them. Without hesitation, she said yes.

Building up a spy network

Bettignies was given a false identity card showing the name Alice Dubois. She sailed for Holland. From there she was smuggled through Belgium and back into France. Bettignies contacted old friends around the Lille area, and one by one asked them to join her in her work. This way she built up a large spy network. It became known as the Alice Service.

The work was dangerous. German soldiers patrolled the border between Belgium and Holland, and would not let anyone cross. Bettignies managed to cross it secretly almost every week. She carried important information to British agents on the other side.

Louise de Bettignies, a frail young woman who became a master spy.

Hiding secrets

Bettignies moved around Lille, gathering and delivering reports from other spies. German soldiers often stopped and searched her. She hid secret reports in many clever places, such as in children's toys and candy bars, or on the backs of postage stamps. One time, she hid a message right in front of everyone's eyes. She had a report copied in tiny writing in invisible ink onto transparent paper, and then glued that paper over the lenses of her glasses.

The Western Front

A major battle line called the Western Front crossed northern France near Lille. The Alice Service worked on the German side of this battle line, and sent hundreds of valuable reports to the British about the state of the German army. After each battle, Bettignies would count the troop trains taking wounded soldiers back to Germany. This simple information helped the British work out how many German soldiers were being lost.

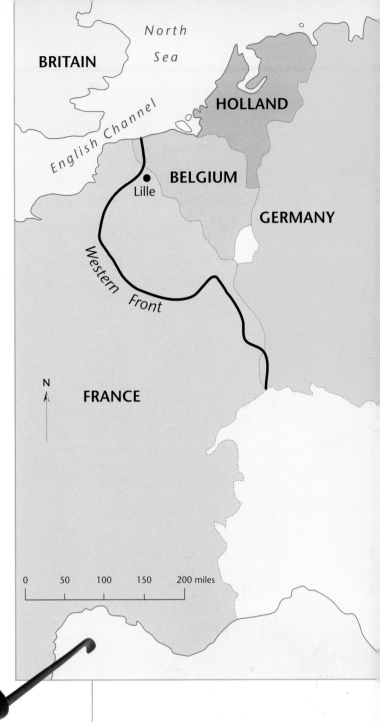

Found out!

The Germans found out about the Alice Service. Slowly they tracked down its agents. To keep her friends safe, Bettignies closed down the network but continued to spy on her own. In September 1915, Bettignies was arrested. She swallowed the secret message she was carrying. The Germans had no proof that she was a spy, but they sent her to prison anyway. Louise de Bettignies died in prison, just two months before the war ended in 1918.

spy network	a group of spies working together
transparent	can been seen through

BACKGROUND

- Towards the end of World War I, there was a workers' revolution in Russia.

- The revolutionaries assassinated the Russian Tsar and set up a communist government.

- Britain was worried that this new communist revolution might spread through Europe.

Sidney Reilly.

Sigmund Rosenblum, known as **Sidney Reilly**: 1874–1925(?)
Born: Odessa, Russia
Spied mainly for Britain against Germany and Russia

Reilly's early days

Sidney Reilly was a teenager when he stowed away on a ship to South America. First he worked as a laborer. Then he got a job as a cook for a British expedition to Brazil. Reilly was a good cook, and a good shot with a rifle. When the expedition was attacked by Brazilian indigenous people, Reilly's sharp-shooting was able to scare them off. The leader of the expedition was a British secret service major. He gave Reilly money to pay for his passage back to Britain. He also gave Reilly an introduction to the secret service.

Spying in Manchuria, Russia, and Germany

Reilly began spying at the age of 22. In Manchuria, he spied for the Japanese. He pretended to be a dock worker and gathered information about Russian ships. Next, Reilly worked for the Russian Tsar. In St. Petersburg, Reilly gathered information about the revolutionaries. In return, the Tsar gave him a beautiful apartment full of priceless art. Reilly then worked in Krupp's gun factory in Germany during the day. At night, he stole plans for German weapons.

Reilly's Russian plot

Soon after a communist government was set up in Russia, the British got Reilly to sneak in under cover. His job was to stop the spread of communism by secretly assassinating the communist leader, Vladimir Ilich Lenin. Reilly bribed two of Lenin's bodyguards to betray their leader when the time was right.

A few days before this was to happen, Lenin gave a speech to workers in a factory. A mad woman in the crowd thought that Lenin was the old Russian Tsar. She pulled out a pistol and shot him. Lenin was only wounded. He had his bodyguards arrested because they should have saved him. The bodyguards confessed to plotting with Reilly, and Reilly was lucky to escape.

Betrayed by The Trust

In 1920, a secret group called The Trust was formed. It was made up of Russians who wished to overthrow Lenin and the communist government. Reilly volunteered to make one last trip into Russia to contact this group and try to help them in any way he could. The Trust turned out to be a clever trick set up by the communist secret police. They caught Reilly and put him in prison. Reilly was never seen again. Some reports say that he was shot, and others say that he escaped. No one knows what happened to him.

The leader of the Russian revolution, Lenin, giving a speech in a Russian street.

assassinated   murdered for a political cause

communist government a government where voters can elect people from only one political party

revolution   a big change that affects a large number of people

sharp-shooting   skills in using a gun

under cover   pretending to be someone else

JULIUS SILBER, THE PERFECT SPY

Julius Silber: 1875–1933
Born: Silesia, in the German empire
Spied for Germany against Britain

Silber offers to become a spy

Julius Silber was working as a businessman in the U.S. when World War I started. Silber spoke perfect English, so he offered to become a spy for his homeland, Germany. He was quickly smuggled into Britain. There he soon got a job as a censor in the British post office.

"PASSED BY CENSOR"

Silber sat at a desk, opening and reading mail all day. The job was not exciting, but he was able to help his country in many different ways. He made sure that the letters of other German spies got through to their spy chiefs in Holland. If Silber read a letter that contained something useful to the British, he held onto it for a few days. This way, the important information often arrived too late to be of use. Other times, Silber smudged part of a letter so that the important words could not be read. No one suspected what he was doing. When Silber stamped the envelopes "PASSED BY CENSOR," the letters inside would not be looked at again.

BRITAIN
HOLLAND
London
GERMAN EMPIRE
SILESIA
AUSTRIA-HUNGARY
N
0   300 miles

A secret room

Silber often found important information in letters, but he never wrote it down at work or in his room at the boarding house. Instead, he rented another room on the other side of London. There he wrote his reports or photographed documents sneaked out of the censor's office. Silber took no risks. He knew that the people in the boarding house where he lived would wonder what he did on his evenings away. To avoid suspicion, he left theater tickets and café checks lying about in his room for the landlady to find.

False walls fold down to reveal the hidden gun on this British merchant ship. The man on board is a disguised officer.

An important discovery

One day, Silber opened a letter from a young lady. It told of special work her brother was doing, refitting old merchant ships. Silber took the afternoon off work and visited the young lady. He showed her the letter, and warned her that she could go to prison for writing about such things. He asked her how much she knew. She told him everything. She said the British were hiding guns in merchant ships so they could sink German submarines. Silber got this news to his spy chief straight away.

Merchant ships on which guns were hidden.

Surprise

When the war ended in 1918, Silber returned to Germany and wrote a book about being a spy. This was how the British learned of his spying activities.

landlady   a woman who rents rooms in her home for people to live in

merchant ships   unarmed ships that carry cargo

MARIA DE VICTORICA, THE SOUTH AMERICAN SPY QUEEN

BACKGROUND

? The U.S. joined World War I on February 3, 1917, and fought on the side of Britain and the Allies.

? Argentina sided with Germany and the Central Powers, but it did not join in the war.

Maria de Victorica: 1882–1920
Born: Buenos Aires, Argentina
Spied for Germany against Britain and the U.S.

Preparing for life as a spy

At the age of 19, Maria de Victorica left Argentina and went to Germany to study languages in college. Because she spoke so many languages, the German secret service soon became interested in her. They arranged a special wedding for her. Victorica married a man from Chile, but she never saw the man again after the wedding. By marrying a Chilean man, Victorica got a Chilean passport. This allowed her to travel to Britain and America. Victorica was ready to begin her life as a spy.

The Irish rebels

Victorica's first spy mission was in Ireland. There she helped the Irish rebels in their war against Britain. She got some of the rebels to join the British army, where they secretly put bombs in the holds of ships and poured acid into machinery. Victorica had German guns smuggled into Ireland so that the rebels could wage a full-scale war on Britain. Armed with German weapons, the Irish rebels attacked British troops in the streets of Dublin on Easter Sunday 1916.

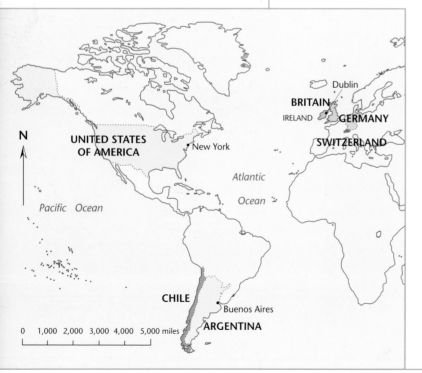

Victorica goes to the U.S.

When the U.S. joined the war, Victorica sailed for New York. There she ran a spy ring that included several bomb makers. To get the materials they needed, Victorica asked a Catholic priest to buy holy statues for her from Switzerland. The priest did not know that the statues were hollow and filled with chemicals for making bombs.

The newspaper switch

Victorica needed a lot of money to run her spy ring, and the money was delivered by couriers. One courier was a schoolgirl who went to St. Patrick's Cathedral in New York every day to pray. The girl carried a rolled-up newspaper. When she left the cathedral, the newspaper was always left behind on the seat. The next courier was an elderly man who also carried a rolled-up newspaper. He sat in the same seat as the girl. Before he left the cathedral, he swapped his newspaper for hers.

American agents spotted this switch one day, and followed the man to a luxury hotel. He left the rolled-up newspaper on a chair, and the next person to pick it up was Victorica. The agents swooped and arrested her. Inside the newspaper was $20,000.

Victorica never stood trial, but went straight to prison. There she became sick. When the war ended, she went to a convent and was cared for by Catholic nuns until her death.

St. Patrick's Cathedral in New York, where the newspaper switch took place.

couriers   people who deliver messages or goods

FRANZ VON RINTELEN, THE MAD BOMBER

Franz von Rintelen: 1877–1949
Born: Germany
Spied for Germany against the U.S.

Buy it or blow it up

Franz von Rintelen went to the U.S. in 1915. He used a false passport bearing the name Emile V. Gasche. Arriving in New York, he set up an export business. His real mission was to buy supplies of food and guns so that they could not be sent to the Allies. Rintelen soon saw that it would be easier, and cheaper, just to blow up the supplies. Rintelen met with his spy chief and outlined a daring plan to blow up ships and warehouses—even whole harbors. His spy chief thought he was mad.

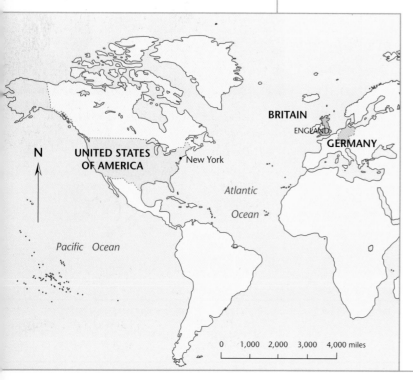

The bomb factory

Several German ships had been interned in New York Harbor for the war. Rintelen secretly visited one of these ships, and got the German crew to turn the ship into a bomb factory. Rintelen designed the bombs himself, and the crew secretly made them. One bomb looked like a small length of pipe. Rintelen got Irish dock workers to plant these bombs in the holds of ships. He blew up 35 ships this way.

Rintelen's cleverest trick

Rintelen helped start a group called Labor's National Peace Council. This was a group of Americans who did not want their country to go to war. They tried to get the government to stop sending guns to the Allies in Europe. The Peace Council urged workers in gun factories to go on strike. They urged dock workers to refuse to load ships with supplies for Allied soldiers. The Peace Council leaders did not know that they were being helped with money from Germany.

Time to leave

The whole time he was in the U.S. Rintelen was followed by British agents. He was careful not to get caught. His schemes were often reckless, but he was not. When some of his bomb makers were arrested, Rintelen decided it was time to leave. He boarded a Dutch ship bound for Europe. However, when the ship stopped in England, Rintelen was arrested by the British. They had cracked the code that Rintelen's spy chief used to send messages. These messages proved that he was a spy. Rintelen spent one year in a British prison and another year in an American prison. He liked England, and returned to live there after the war ended.

The initials E.V.G.

Rintelen used many false names while he was spying in America: Emile V. Gasche, Edward V. Gates, and E.V. Gibbons. No one knows why he always liked to use E.V.G. for his initials.

Captain von Rintelen.

A U.S. ship carrying supplies for the Allies. These ships were prime targets for Rintelen's bombers.

export   to send goods out of the country

interned   imprisoned or held during a time of war

MARTHE RICHER, THE DOUBLE AGENT

Marthe Richer: 1889–1950
Born: Lorraine, France
Spied for France against Germany

BACKGROUND

- Spain was a neutral country in World War I. It did not join the fighting.

- Many spies for both sides worked in and out of Spain.

Marthe Richer, double agent.

A happy life

Marthe Richer was born in the Lorraine district of France, close to the German border. She studied German at school and spoke the language fluently. When Richer left school at age 17, she set up a store in Paris selling ladies' clothes. At 22, she became one of the first women in France to learn to fly a plane. Richer was a bright young woman who led a happy life.

Grief

Richer married a French military officer in 1914. He was killed in action just one year later. Richer decided to become a spy to help herself get over her sadness, and also to help France.

Life as a spy in Spain

Three weeks after her husband's death, Richer went to the seaside town of San Sebastian in Spain. There she went to parties and wore fashionable clothes. Richer told everyone that because she was from Lorraine, she was really more German than French. The German secret service in Spain soon asked Richer if she would spy for them. This was exactly what her French spy chief had hoped would happen.

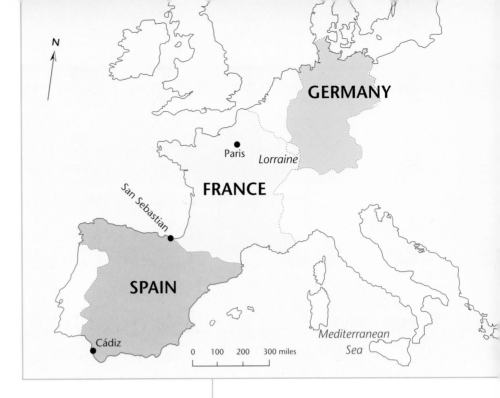

Back and forth

The Germans asked Richer to go back to France and get information about certain weapons being made in a Paris factory. Richer was given invisible ink for writing secret reports. She went straight to the French secret service in Paris. The French were pleased to have a sample of Germany's latest invisible ink. The French gave Richer false information about the gun factory to take back to the Germans. The Germans believed it was true. Richer became a trusted German agent. All the time she was a double agent, loyal to the French.

Amazing secrets

Richer became close friends with the German secret service chief in Spain. One day, he took her to see a German submarine in Cádiz Harbor. Richer took note of everything she saw in the submarine. The French were amazed when they received her detailed report.

The medal of honor

Richer returned to France when the war ended in 1918. She gave the French government all the money the Germans had paid her for spying. She had done such a good job as a double agent that many people in France believed she truly had spied for Germany. It was not until 15 years after the war that Richer was finally given a medal for her service to her country. She received France's highest award, the Legion of Honor.

fluently   quickly and easily

WILHELM WASSMUSS, THE GOLDEN SPY

BACKGROUND

❓ The oilfields of Persia (now called Iran) produced fuel that was important to Britain in World War I.

❓ Britain sent soldiers to Persia to try to keep the oilfields safe from Germany and Turkey.

Wilhelm Wassmuss, German consul in Persia.

Wilhelm Wassmuss: 1880–1931
Born: Hanover, Germany
Spied for Germany against Britain

Wassmuss dreams of adventure

When Wilhelm Wassmuss was a boy, he dreamed of traveling to exciting countries and having great adventures. His dreams came true when he got a job in the German embassy in Persia. Wassmuss was fascinated by the Persian tribes. He quickly learned their customs and their languages. When World War I broke out in 1914, all the German people working in Persia were sent home. Wassmuss asked to stay on.

Bold plans

Wassmuss saw that it would help Germany if he could persuade some of the Persian tribes to make war on the British. The German government liked this idea, and offered to send Wassmuss all the gold he might need. Wassmuss then printed leaflets telling the Persians that the British were the enemy of their religious leader, the caliph of Islam. This caused the Persians to declare a *jihad*, or holy war, against Britain. Wassmuss gave the Persian tribesmen gold to buy guns and horses. The Persians were good fighters, and they soon cut Britain's important oil pipeline.

A narrow escape

Britain fought back. British troops were sent to capture the seaport of Bushehr, where Wassmuss lived. The first Wassmuss knew of this attack was when he heard the sound of gunfire in the night. Leaping from his bed, he ordered his servant to load the car with the chests of gold and drive off. Wassmuss jumped on a horse and fled into the hills, still dressed in his silk pajamas. He escaped only with his life and his gold. Wassmuss left behind a copy of a German code book. With this book, the British were able to decode every message sent by the Germans for the next three years.

TURKEY

IRAN (Persia)

Bushehr

SAUDI ARABIA

Persian Gulf

0   250   500   750 miles

Gold and lies

In 1917, the war started to go badly for Germany and the Persians were not so willing to fight. Wassmuss told them lies. He said that Germany had already invaded England and taken the English king prisoner. Next, Wassmuss said that the English king had been executed in a public square. A little later, Wassmuss reported that Russia had surrendered to Germany. None of this was true, but these lies kept the Persians fighting for Wassmuss even after the gold ran out.

Debts to pay

By 1918, even the Persians in their mountain caves knew that Germany was defeated. Wassmuss went back to Germany to try to get the gold he still owed the tribesmen. Germany was ruined. Wassmuss used his own money to make the payments he had promised.

Wassmuss traveled about with chests full of gold.

decode   to change a secret message back into plain text

embassy   a building where officials from another country work and sometimes live

ELSBETH SCHRAGMÜLLER, THE SPY TEACHER

Elsbeth Schragmüller: 1887–1940
Born: Westphalia, Germany
Trained spies for Germany against Britain and France

BACKGROUND

When World War I started in 1914, most German spies in Britain and France were arrested and put in prison.

Germany needed more spies, but the spies had to be trained before they could be sent into the field.

code name   a simple name used to hide the identity of a spy

Eager to be a spy

Elsbeth Schragmüller was a university teacher when World War I began. She wrote to the chief of German military intelligence and asked to work for him. Schragmüller was sent to the Baden-Baden spy school. She passed her exams with such high marks that it was decided she should become a spy teacher. She was too good to risk in the field.

Fräulein Doktor and the Antwerp spy school

Schragmüller went to teach in a German spy school in Antwerp, Belgium. There, German spies were trained for work in Britain and France. Each student had a small room. The shutters on the windows were always locked. For the first three weeks, the students had all their lessons and meals in their rooms. Students and teachers wore masks to hide their faces, and everyone used a code name. Students were not allowed to make friends with one another. Schragmüller taught hundreds of spies in the Antwerp school. Her students called her *Fräulein Doktor,* which means "Miss Doctor" or female doctor.

After the war

Schragmüller went back to Germany in 1918 and taught history in Munich University. Most Germans had heard of the famous *Fräulein Doktor,* but very few people knew who she was.

GLOSSARY

archaeological diggings places where ancient cities are dug up and studied

assassinated murdered for a political cause

ciphers secret languages that hide words by jumbling their letters

code name a simple name used to hide the identity of a spy

codes secret languages

communist government a government where voters can elect people from only one political party

couriers people who deliver messages or goods

decode to change a secret message back into plain text

disguised when a person's appearance is changed so they look like someone else

double agent a spy pretending to work for one country while secretly working for another

Dutch belonging to Holland

embassy a building where officials from another country work and sometimes live

export to send goods out of the country

fluently quickly and easily

gadgets special tools

identity cards official cards with a person's name and photograph that prove who they are

inlet a strip of water stretching into the land from the sea

interned imprisoned or held during a time of war

into the field going into other countries to spy

invaded used force to enter someone else's land

landlady a woman who rents rooms in her home for people to live in

line of supply route along which supplies are transported

matron person in charge of nurses in a hospital

merchant ships unarmed ships that carry cargo

military the armed forces

ocean liner a luxury passenger ship

passport an official identification document needed by someone traveling to another country

revolution a big change that affects a large number of people

secret service another name for a spy network

sharp-shooting skills in using a gun

spy chief a person in charge of other spies

spy network a group of spies working together

transparent can been seen through

under cover pretending to be someone else

INDEX